Best Wishes – a joy to meet you. Keep teaching!
Carolyn

Dear Hannah,

May you grow up
to see around all
sides of the Truth.

Michael
Karlberg

ROOTH SEES A TROOTH

Written by: **Michael Karlberg**

Illustrations by: **Craig Howarth**

Rooth Sees a Trooth

Illustrations: Craig Howarth
Book Layout and Cover Design: Mariya Daliri

First Edition 2007
ISBN 1 876322 16 0

Distributed by
Bahá'í Distribution Services
P.O. Box 300 Bundoora
Vic. 3083 Australia

HYPERLINK "mailto:bds@bnc.bahai.org.au" bds@bahai.org.au
HYPERLINK "http://www.bahaibooks.com" www.bahaibooks.com

"This book is dedicated to my daughters, *Leah* and *Jessa*,
for whom the story was first written."

In a far away land there's an **odd little nation**
where **plain common sense** has gone on vacation.
In this odd little nation they **never** agree.
It's a strange little **quirk** of the way that they see.
Half see from the **left**, half see from the **right**.
Each half of **them** sees just the **opposite sight**.,

Now this **state of affairs** may seem a bit strange.
As a matter of fact, it's hard to **explain**.
It's **somehow** related to how much they earn,
the way that they talk, and the way that they learn.
You see, **right-looking** kids go to right-looking schools
where they study and practice their right-looking **rules**.
While **left-looking** kids learn that left-looking's **best**
as they study and practice for **left-looking** tests.

After school all the **right**-lookers watch their **TVs**,
but **right**-looking **channels** are all that they see.
While **left**-lookers **listen** to left-looking **views**
on channels with round-the-clock **left**-looking **news**.

In the summertime, right-lookers all go to **camps**
to sing right-looking **songs**, collect right-looking **stamps**.

While left-looking **campers** hum left-looking **tunes** and **trade** left-looking **stamps** in the late afternoons.

When the children grow up, they go and get **jobs**
pushing right-sided **buttons** or left-sided **knobs**.
Then everyone marries the **same-looking** kin
to begin the whole **cycle** all over again.
And so they each keep to their different groups,
except when they gather to argue about...

... Trooths.

You see Trooths are **strange creatures**,
they're really a **sight**.
They're **blue** on the left, they're **green** on the right.
The blue side has **feathers**, the green side has **scales**.
The left side has **claws**, the right side has **nails**.
On the top of their head grows thick shaggy hair.
But **one side** is dark, **the other** side fair.
And under each ear, an ear-ring hangs down.
On one ear it's **red**, on the other it's **brown**.

So the trouble with Trooths is they don't **look the same**
from the left to the right, no **features** remain.
And the troubles are **double** in this odd little nation
where plain common sense has gone on **vacation**.
For a Trooth **looks** so different through a right-looking **eye**,
that left-lookers think all the right-lookers **lie**.
Yet when Trooths are described by the left-looking kind,
the right-lookers claim that the lefties are **blind**.

Yes they only look **one way**, that's just how they see.
And this is the **reason** they never agree.
So they argue 'bout Trooths every chance that they get.
When it's hot and it's dry, when it's rainy and wet.
They argue **whenever** they meet in the street.
They argue until they can't stand on their feet.

They've argued so long that they've made **institutions**
where they argue non-stop in their **search** for solutions
to problems that rise from the **ways** that they see –
because **nothing** gets done when they never agree.
So for **years and for years**, they've argued 'bout Trooths.

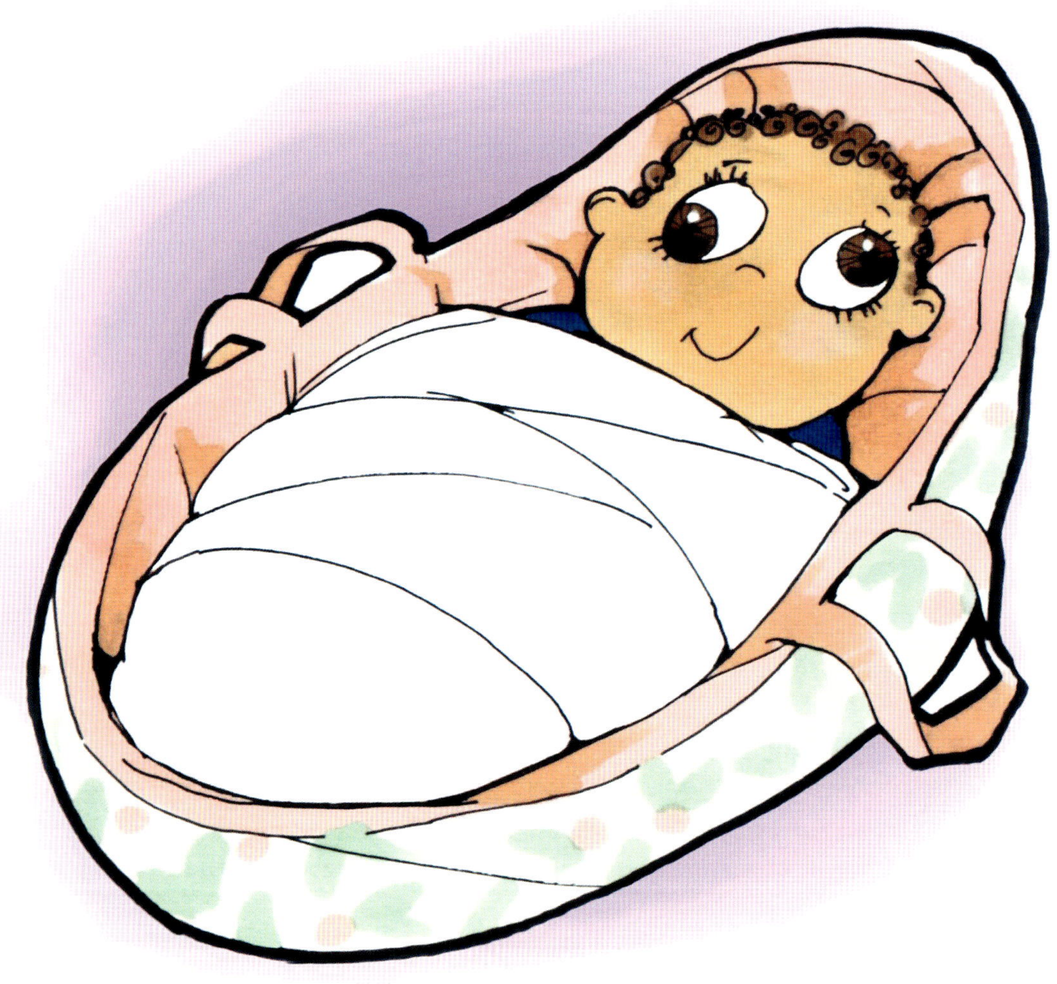

Until one day a child was **born**, named...

As Rooth went on, a **crowd** started to gather.
Until finally the **mayor** came to ask
"What's the matter?"

"**This** girl", the crowd said, "**is right out of her mind!**

Either that or the poor girl is totally blind!

She claims that this Trooth has **two sides** that are **different**.

That one side is one way, the other side isn't.

She claims it depends on **which view** that you take.

That by looking **just one way** we've made a **mistake**.

She claims that if **everyone looked** right around.

We'd see all the **same things** that she said she found."

"**Humph!**" humphed the **mayor**.
"**That's simply absurd!**
That's the silliest **nonsense** that I've ever **heard!**
Little girl, you need help, you must be **quite ill**.
Let's go find a **doctor**, to give you a pill."

"**Oh** no," pleaded Rooth, "I'm seeing **quite clearly**.
And you'll see **what I see**, if you stand here near me."
But the mayor refused, for he could not **admit**
that in seeing the Trooth he saw only a **bit**.

As he **humphed** once again, in a voice that was proud,
a left-looking lad wandered out from the **crowd.**
"**She's right!**" the boy squeaked, as he stepped up to look.
"**I've never seen** this in my **left-looking book!**"
In turn, a small **right-looking boy** stepped up too.
"**Oh yes,** all the things that she said are quite **true!**"
With that, all the kids went to take their **own** peek.
And they got so **excited**, they hardly could **speak.**

But the **parents** stood back, to the left and the right,
not wanting to look, afraid of the sight.
'Cause they learned all their lives **to see just one way.**
And if they learned **wrong**, then what could they say?
"**Kids** they insisted, **don't listen to Rooth!**"
Step back, they persisted, **don't look at that Trooth!**
You've all been **confused**, or you're under a **spell**,
or you must have **been tricked**, or you're **not** feeling well."

They gathered their children and led them all home
and **poor little Rooth**, was left standing **alone**.
Alone with the Trooth, and **no one** to tell.
Now poor little Rooth really **didn't feel well**.

So Rooth went home too, and she **crawled** into bed,
and she **pulled** all the blankets up **over her head**.
She snuggled up tight and **sighed** a **big sigh**.
She pondered and puzzled and asked herself "**Why?**"
"**Oh why won't they listen**? Oh why won't they **see**?
What's keeping them back? **How hard can it be?**"
But they just couldn't do it – the **adults** at least.
Couldn't listen nor **look** 'round all sides of that beast.
For the adults, **alas**, were too **set** in their **views**.
They were **trained to look one way**
– that's all they could do.

Then deep down inside, Rooth felt something **stir**.
"The kids!" she **remembered**, had **been there with her**.
They **saw** what she **saw** and they **knew** what she **knew**.
They had all **looked both ways** so they knew
it was true.

Yes the kids all remember, and one day, no doubt,
the truth about Trooths will surely come out.
The kids haven't forgotten – they won't, you can bet.
For both sides of a Trooth, are hard to forget.